Impressum / legal notice
© Copyright 2019
1. Auflage / 1. Edition
alle Rechte vorbehalten
all rights reserved

Kontakt / contact:
Fernando Carrillo Castillo
Am Fackelstein 3a
56305 Puderbach, Germany

Covergestaltung / cover design:
Fernando Carrillo Castillo

www.ingramcontent.com/pod-product-compliance
Lightning Source LLC
Chambersburg PA
CBHW070659220526
45466CB00001B/498